Contents

Basking shark

The basking shark is one of the biggest fish in the world. It swims along with its mouth open.

> « Every hour, up to 7000 gallons of water passes through a basking shark's mouth!

My Little Book of
Sharks

by Camilla de la Bédoyère

QED

Designed, edited and picture researched by Starry Dog Books Ltd

First published in the UK in 2015 by
QED Publishing
Part of The Quarto Group
The Old Brewery,
6 Blundell Street,
London,
N7 9BH

www.qed-publishing.co.uk

A catalogue record for this book is available from the British Library.

ISBN 978 1 78171 989 3

Printed in China

Words in **bold** are
explained in the
glossary on page 60.

>> **Basking sharks can grow up to 12 metres long.**

^ **Basking sharks have very long** gill slits. **They use these to breathe.**

Females swim near the surface of the water. Males swim in deeper water. They feed on small animals called **plankton**.

Basking sharks are harmless to humans. They have tiny teeth.

5

Whale shark

Whale sharks are the biggest fish in the world, but they only eat small animals.

⌄ **Every whale shark has its own pattern of spots and stripes.**

« **Adult whale sharks usually grow to about 12 metres long.**

» **Whale sharks eat tiny creatures, such as small** squid**, shrimps, fish and fish eggs.**

This shark swims with its mouth open. Water flows in and passes through sievelike plates that trap food. It then flows out through the shark's **gills**.

Lemon shark

Lemon sharks get their name from their yellowy skin. They live in warm, shallow water around **coral reefs**.

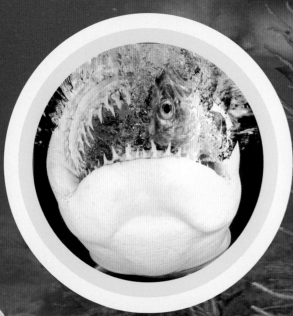

<< This lemon shark has caught a fish with its rows of very sharp teeth.

At night lemon sharks swim and hunt for food. They eat fish, small sharks, squid and **crustaceans**. They even attack seabirds!

˅ Remora fish attach themselves to lemon sharks. They eat scraps of food that the sharks drop.

ʌ During the day, lemon sharks rest near the seabed.

Whitetip reef shark

The shark's mouth is on the underside of its head, so it can eat animals on the seabed.

Whitetip reef sharks are small, shy animals. They are named after the white tips on their **fins**.

» These sharks often stay near the seabed.

Most sharks live alone, but whitetip reef sharks often hunt at night in groups. They stay near caves, rocks and underwater cliffs, where they look for crustaceans and fish to eat.

^ These whitetip reef sharks can smell food!

Grey reef shark

Grey reef sharks live in large groups, in clear waters around coral reefs. They are fast swimmers.

⌃ The small holes on a shark's snout help it sense when other animals are nearby.

To scare other animals – or humans – away, a grey reef shark does some special moves. It rolls around, arches its back and lifts its **snout**.

⌃ A group of sharks is called a school.

⌃ Grey reef sharks are usually less than 150 centimetres long.

Sandtiger shark

Sandtiger sharks are also called ragged-tooth sharks. They have long, spiky teeth!

⌄ **Sandtiger sharks are slow, strong swimmers.**

« **A sandtiger's teeth are the perfect size and shape for gripping slippery fish.**

Sandtigers grow to more than 4 metres long. They hunt in groups of up to 80 sharks. These sharks often swim close to sandy shores.

⌃ This hungry sandtiger shark is hunting for small fish to eat.

Tiger shark

Tiger sharks are dangerous. They are fast swimmers and are very powerful.

˅ **Young tiger sharks have spots. Adults have stripes.**

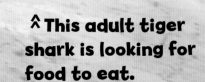

^ **This adult tiger shark is looking for food to eat.**

A tiger shark's favorite foods are fish, seabirds and turtles.

>> A tiger shark's teeth are serrated, like the blade of a saw.

These aggressive sharks sometimes attack people too.

Bull shark

Most sharks spend all of their lives in the sea, but bull sharks can also live in rivers.

⌄ **These** predators **have big, heavy bodies and broad snouts.**

⌃ **Bull sharks have small eyes, but a very good sense of smell.**

Bull sharks are some of the world's most dangerous sharks. They live in rivers and shallow seas, where people often swim, wash or fish.

>> A bull shark's teeth are dagger-shaped and are arranged in rows.

Broadnose sevengill shark

Most sharks have five pairs of gill slits, but these sharks have seven pairs instead.

>> Broadnose sevengill sharks can grow to about 3 metres long.

⌄ **These sharks are fast swimmers, with long, powerful tails.**

Broadnose sevengill sharks live in cool, shallow water near land and hunt for fish, seals and small whales to eat.

^ These sharks often have white and black speckles on their skin.

Blacktip reef shark

Coral reefs provide a good **habitat** for blacktip reef sharks. The reefs are home to plenty of small animals for the sharks to hunt.

˅ A coral reef is an ocean habitat made up of tiny animals called coral polyps.

« This shark's dorsal fin **has a black tip.**

Blacktip reef sharks live in warm, shallow waters. They eat fish, squid and crustaceans.

These sharks swim away quickly if they are disturbed.

^ These reef sharks often gather in groups near the shore.

Great white shark

This is one of the world's most amazing animals. It is big, strong and deadly.

⌃ The biggest great white sharks are 6 metres long!

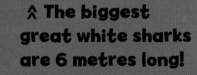

« A great white shark is so strong it can leap out of the water.

>> Great white sharks have about 300 teeth.

Great white sharks hunt large animals. They swim fast and catch seals, tuna and dolphins to eat. These sharks go on long journeys across the oceans.

Shortfin mako

The shortfin mako is the fastest shark in the world. It can leap out of the water and swim long distances.

⌄ **Fast sharks have long, tube-shaped bodies that slice through the water.**

>> **Shortfin makos have long, smooth teeth with sharp points.**

Shortfin makos can swim nearly 2000 kilometres in less than 40 days.

These predators need to swim fast to catch their speedy **prey**, which include tuna and swordfish.

ᐱ Tunas are big. One tuna may be more than half the size of a shortfin mako.

Porbeagle

Most porbeagles live in the North Atlantic Ocean. They can grow to more than 3 metres long.

⌄ **Porbeagles have good eyesight and may even see some colours.**

« **A shark's dorsal fin stops it from rolling on its side as it swims.**

<< Each tooth has a large, bladelike part, and a 'mini-tooth' on each side of it.

Fish – including most sharks – have cold bodies, but porbeagles keep their muscles warm. This means they can live in cold seas and swim fast to chase their prey.

Thresher shark

There are three **species** of thresher shark. This is a pelagic thresher shark. It lives in the Indian and Pacific Oceans.

∧ **This shark is a shiny copper colour on top, mixed with blue.**

« **Thresher sharks have long** pectoral fins.

>> Half of this shark's length is its tail!

These sharks have large eyes and small mouths. They use their very long tails to hit and stun fish before eating them.

Blue shark

These are the most graceful of all sharks. Blue sharks live in the open ocean, in warm and cool waters.

ꕦ **Blue sharks swim near the surface, looking for fish to eat.**

>> This predator feeds on shoals of fish, such as anchovies.

Blue sharks go on long journeys, called migrations. They can travel thousands of kilometres across the ocean because their bodies are **streamlined**.

Silky shark

Silky sharks are large sharks with long, pointed snouts and large eyes.

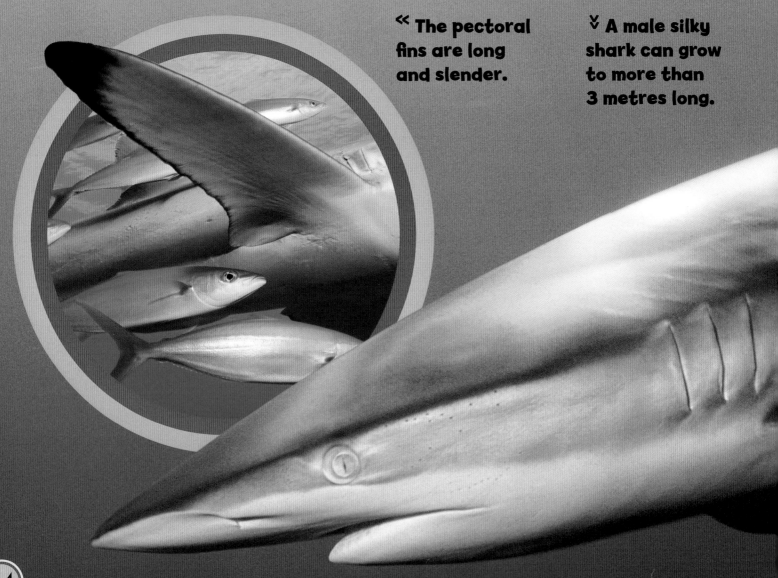

« The pectoral fins are long and slender.

⌄ A male silky shark can grow to more than 3 metres long.

These large predators live in warm, open oceans, anywhere that they can find lots of fish to eat. They are fast swimmers and chase schools of big fish, including tuna and **mackerel**.

>> **When a silky shark is scared, it arches its back and shows its sharp teeth.**

Oceanic whitetip shark

Oceanic whitetip sharks swim in the open ocean, far from land. They grow up to 3 metres long.

Shear Water

« These sharks often swim in groups and follow fishing boats.

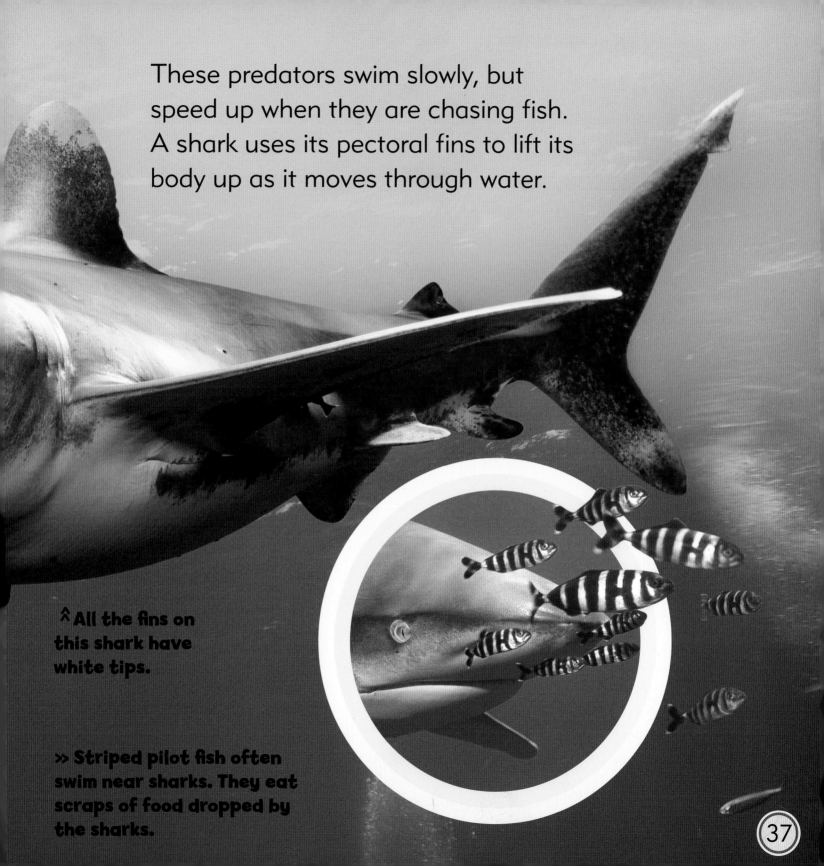

These predators swim slowly, but speed up when they are chasing fish. A shark uses its pectoral fins to lift its body up as it moves through water.

⌃ All the fins on this shark have white tips.

» Striped pilot fish often swim near sharks. They eat scraps of food dropped by the sharks.

Angelshark

Angelsharks have broad, flat bodies. They look more like rays or **skates** than sharks.

>> **Angelsharks are** camouflaged **on the seabed.**

There are about 20 species of angelshark. This species lives in the northeast Atlantic and Mediterranean Sea. Angelsharks are strong swimmers.

⌃ Angelsharks bury themselves in sand. This one is almost invisible!

Spotted wobbegong

Wobbegongs are sometimes called 'carpetsharks', because they look like patterned carpets!

> ⌄Bits of skin hang from this shark's mouth. They help it hide among seaweed.

>> **A spotted wobbegong is almost invisible as it swims near the seabed.**

Wobbegong sharks hunt for lobsters, flat fish and octopuses on the seabed.

There are about 10 species of wobbegong. They live in the Pacific Ocean.

41

Zebra shark

When zebra sharks are young, they have stripes. When they get older, they have spots.

⌄ **Most zebra sharks grow to about 2 metres long.**

^ **Young sharks are called pups. This pup still has its stripes.**

Zebra sharks wriggle inside rocky holes to find small fish and crabs to eat. Their mouths are full of small, spiked teeth.

ᐱ The holes above this shark's small mouth are nostrils.

Port Jackson shark

This shark belongs to a family of fish called bullhead sharks.

⌄ **Adults have dark bands of colour on their skin.**

« **Bullhead sharks hunt for food at night. This one is eating an egg case.**

Port Jackson sharks use their fins to crawl along the seabed, where they hunt for starfish and sea urchins to eat.

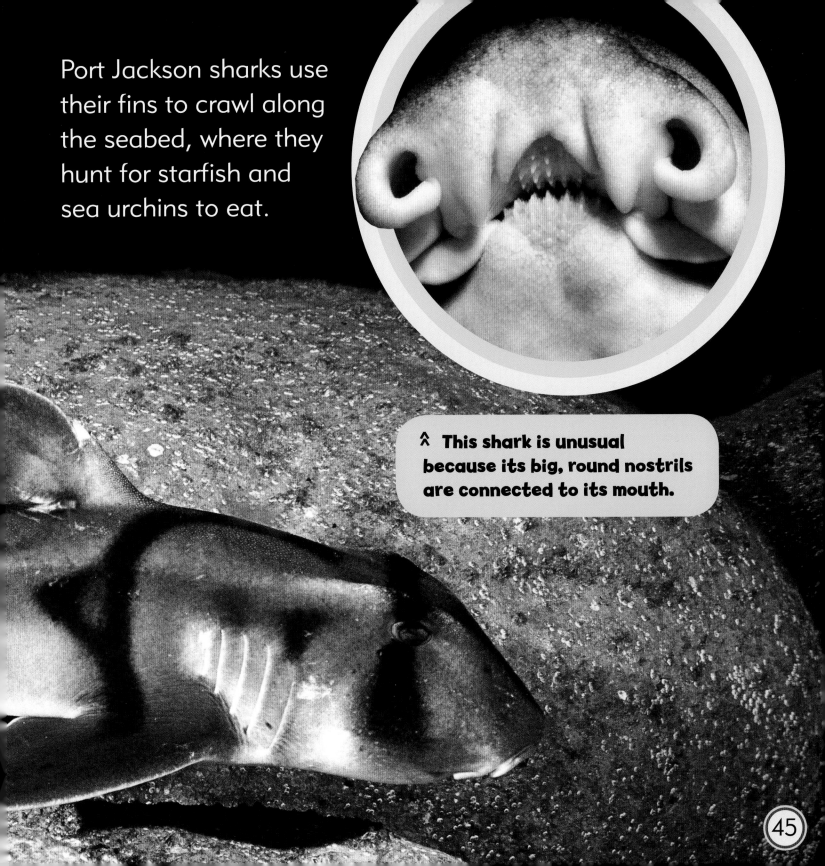

^ This shark is unusual because its big, round nostrils are connected to its mouth.

Swellshark

Swellsharks are also known as puffer sharks or balloon sharks. They have a surprising way of staying safe under the sea!

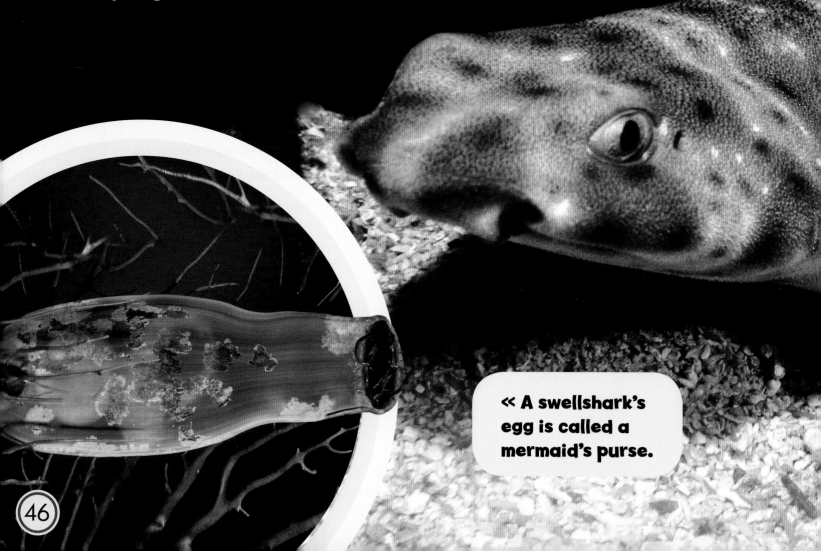

˅ **Most types of swellshark are less than 1 metre long.**

« **A swellshark's egg is called a mermaid's purse.**

∧ **Swellsharks lie on the seabed, waiting for prey to pass by.**

When a swellshark is scared, it gulps water and makes its body swell up to twice its normal size. This scares any predators away.

Epaulette carpetshark

« The shark's snout is a good shape for digging into sand and finding animals to eat.

The epaulette carpetshark lives in warm, shallow seas around the coast of Australia.

This small, shy shark is a slow swimmer. During the day it hides among coral reefs. At night it hunts for animals on the seabed.

˅ This shark has two large spots on its back and a long, thick tail.

>> Carpetsharks use their fins to 'walk' along the seabed.

Greenland shark

Greenland sharks are large, slow and strong. They are also known as sleeper sharks.

≪ Greenland sharks eat squid, fish, seals and any dead animals they find.

˅ A Greenland shark can grow to more than 5 metres long.

These sharks live in cold Arctic waters. They swim slowly, but can turn on a burst of speed when they are hunting.

˄ It is common for Greenland sharks to be blind, especially when they are old.

Great hammerhead

There are about nine species of hammerhead shark. This type is called a great hammerhead.

>> **The dorsal fin is tall and slightly curved.**

^ **Great hammerheads have between 69 and 74 serrated teeth.**

The great
hammerhead uses its
head to quickly swim up or
down, or change direction. It hunts
for small fish, squid and **stingrays**.

Scalloped hammerhead

Hammerhead sharks look strange! Their heads are wide, which makes the sharks hammer-shaped.

>> The shark's eyes are at the ends of its head. This helps it to see predators and find animals to eat.

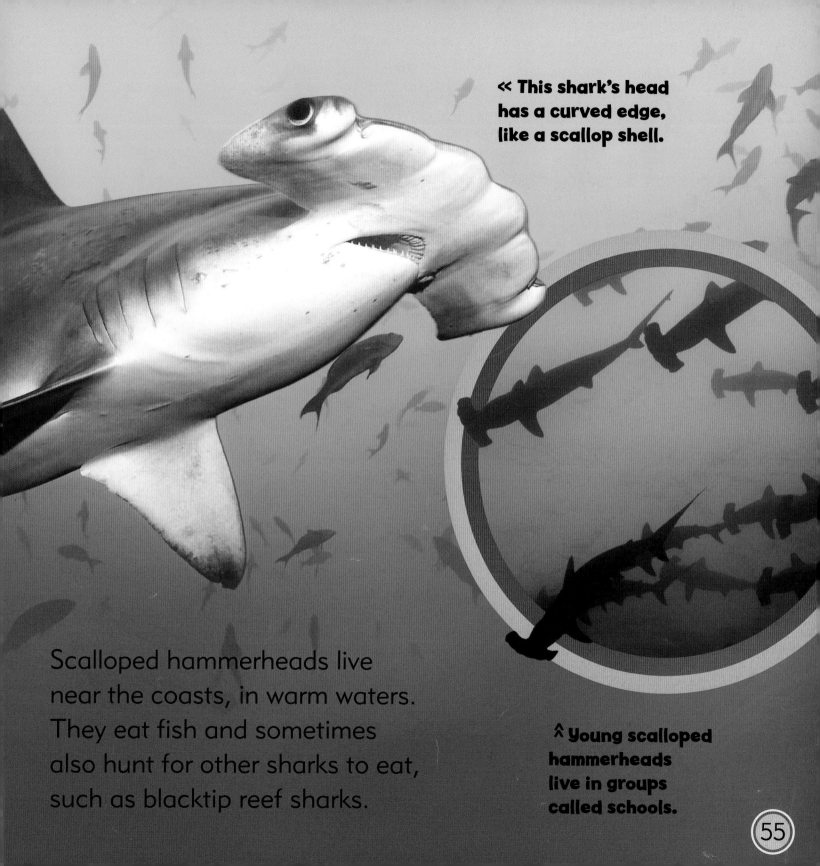

<< This shark's head has a curved edge, like a scallop shell.

Scalloped hammerheads live near the coasts, in warm waters. They eat fish and sometimes also hunt for other sharks to eat, such as blacktip reef sharks.

^ Young scalloped hammerheads live in groups called schools.

Longnose sawshark

A sawshark has a very long, thin snout that is flat and lined with teeth. It uses its snout to swipe at its prey.

∧ **Longnose sawsharks live in Australian waters.**

Sawsharks have poor eyesight and use their **barbels** to touch the seafloor as they swim.

« The shark's mouth is on the underside of its head.

» The shark's barbels are long and sensitive to touch.

Pyjama shark

Pyjama sharks have long, dark stripes. They are also known as striped catsharks.

« Pyjama sharks have a broad, flat head and a blunt snout.

« When a pyjama shark is scared, it rolls its body into a ball.

« Pyjama sharks are usually less than 1 metre long.

During the day, pyjama sharks hide in caves and between rocks. They hunt at night for shelled animals, worms and small fish.

Glossary

barbel A long piece of flesh on a shark's snout. It is used to feel things on the seabed.

camouflage Colours and patterns on an animal that make it hard to spot against its background.

coral reef A rocky place found in warm, shallow seas. Coral reefs are made by little animals called coral polyps.

crustaceans Animals, such as shrimps and crabs, with a tough skin and many legs.

dorsal fin A fin on a shark's back. Most sharks have two.

fin Part of a shark's body that helps it swim.

gills Parts of a shark's body used for breathing.

gill slits Openings on a shark's body that lead to the gills.

habitat The place where an animal lives.

mackerel Small, silvery fish that swim fast.

nostril The hole that leads into a nose or snout.

ocean A huge area of sea, such as the Pacific Ocean.

pectoral fin Fin on a shark's side, just behind its gill slits.

plankton Tiny animals and plants that float in the ocean.

predator An animal that hunts other animals to eat.

prey An animal that is hunted by other animals.

school A group of sharks.

seaweed Plants, also known as algae, that live in the sea.

serrated Having lots of small, sharp points, like the edge of a saw.

skate A type of flat fish.

snout The mouth and nose of an animal.

species A type of animal. A great white shark is a type, or species, of shark.

squid A soft-bodied sea creature closely related to octopuses.

stingray A type of flat fish.

streamlined A smooth shape that is able to move quickly through water.

Index

Picture Credits

(t=top, b=bottom, l=left, r=right, c=centre, fc=front cover, bc=back cover)

Alamy
10-11 © Michael Patrick O'Neill, 16bl © ArteSub, 18-19 © Mark Conlin, 21tr © Kike Calvo/VWPics, 22-23 © Cornforth Images, 28-29 © Doug Perrine, 30tr © Dray van Beeck, 43tr © Erika Antoniazzo, 47cr © Visual&Written SL, 51br © Louise Murray, 56-57 © Stephen Frink Collection, 57tl © Stephen Frink Collection

Corbis Images
52bc © Norbert Wu/Science Faction

Dreamstime
58bl © Anthony Wooldridge

FLPA
11 Fred Bavendam/Minden Pictures, 1r Norbert Wu/Minden Pictures, 7tr Reinhard Dirscherl, 8bl Brandon Cole/Biosphoto, 10cr Colin Marshall, 12-13 Reinhard Dirscherl, 16-17 Norbert Wu/Minden Pictures, 24bl Gerard Lacz, 24-25 Imagebroker, Norbert Probst, Ima/Imagebroker, 25tr Armin Maywald/FN/Minden, 36-37 Norbert Wu/Minden Pictures, 40-41 Fred Bavendam/Minden Pictures, 41tr Pete Oxford/Minden Pictures, 42-43 OceanPhoto, 44bl Fred Bavendam/Minden Pictures, 44-45 Fred Bavendam/Minden Pictures, 46-47 Norbert Wu/Minden Pictures, 48-49 Malcolm Schuyl, 50bl © Tui De Roy/Minden Pictures, 54-55 Norbert Probst/Imagebroker, 57br Kelvin Aitken/Biosphoto

Getty Images
18cl Franco Banfi, 19tr Alexander Safonov, 26br Alberto Pomares, 34l Michele Westmorland, 35br Borut Furlan, 36bl Jim Abernethy, 50-51 Paul Nicklen, 52-53 Brian J. Skerry

Nature Picture Library
2-3 Visuals Unlimited, 4bl Dan Burton, 4-5 Wild Wonders of Europe / Sá, 5tr Dan Burton, 6bl Doug Perrine, 6-7 Doug Perrine, 8-9 Alex Mustard, 9br Alex Mustard, 11cr Jeff Rotman, 12bl Michael Pitts, 13cr Doug Perrine, 14bl Doug Perrine, 14-15 Brandon Cole, 15tr Brandon Cole, 17tl Doug Perrine, 20-21t (circle) Doug Perrine, 22br Cheryl-Samantha Owen, 28cl Doug Perrine, 29tl Doug Perrine, 31t Doug Perrine, 32-33 Nuno Sa, 33t Chris & Monique Fallows, 34-35 Doug Perrine, 37br Michael Pitts, 39r Alex Mustard, 42cl Jurgen Freund, 45tr Jeff Rotman, 46bl Visuals Unlimited, 48c Jeff Rotman, 49br Brandon Cole, 54bc Jeff Rotman, 55cr Brandon Cole, 58-59 Doug Perrine, 59tl Cheryl-Samantha Owen

Photoshot
20-21 © NHPA, 23tr © Picture Alliance/ F. Schneider, 26-27 © Cultura, 38-39 © Picture Alliance/ P. Sutter

Science Photo Library
30-31 Scubazoo

Shutterstock
27br Ugo Montaldo, 49br Iliuta Goean, 60t cbpix, 64br Nikolai Pozdeev